Books in the

Let's Ask Auntie Anne Series

Book One
How to Raise a Loving Child

Book Two
How to Raise a Responsible Child

Book Three
How to Raise a Secure Child

Book Four
How to Raise a Trusting Child

Book Five
How to Raise a Moral Child

Let's Ask Auntie Anne

How to Raise a Loving Child

Book One

Gary and Anne Marie Ezzo
with Diane Wiggins

Let's Ask Auntie Anne
How to Raise A Loving Child

Published by Parent-Wise Solutions, Inc. *(Parent-Wise Solutions is a division of the Charleston Publishing Group, Inc.)*

© 2004 by Gary Ezzo and Anne Marie Ezzo
with Diane Wiggins
Illustrations by Cynthia Gardner
pixelworksstudio.net

International Standard Book Number:

1-932740-05-8

Printed in the United States of America

For information:
Parent-Wise Solutions, Inc.
2130 Cheswick Lane, Mt. Pleasant, SC 29466

04 05 06 07—7 6 5 4 3 2 1

Dedicated to…

Kara
No hug as precious, no smile as warm,
no face as sweet, no heart as gentle
as that of our Kar-Bear

Acknowledgements

Books are often a collaborative effort of many individuals whose gifts and talents help move a manuscript from scribbles to completion. This little book and the entire *Auntie Anne* series is no exception. We are indebted to a host of friends. First, we wish to thank Craig, Carly, Morgan, and Evan Wiggins for allowing wife and Mom time to work on the Auntie Anne series. Their sacrifice gave Diane the opportunity to use her creative giftedness. We also offer a hearty thank you to our wonderful editors Judith St. Pierre and Jennifer Gott. Joining them in proof reading is our dear friend Suzanne Johns and family. Many thanks are offered to Judson Swihart. In his book, How to Say "*I Love You*," (Downer's Grove, IL: Inter-Varsity Press, 1972), Mr. Swihart puts forth the core concepts that echoed in Auntie Anne's presentation. His thoughts are augmented by the work of Dr. Gary Chapman and his book, "*The Five Love Languages*," (Northfield Press: Chicago, 1992). And last but not least, the one who inspired the completion of the series is our beloved Auntie Anne. May her Scrabble board never grow cold.

Series Prologue

Author's Notes

Meet the Real Auntie Anne

Meet the Carriage Couples

Author's Notes

In this series of books we depart from our traditional method of dialectic instruction, (premise, facts, argument and conclusion) and turn to an older and more personal style of persuasion—sharing parenting principles in story-form. Who doesn't love a good story?

Stories are entertaining and provide a unique conduit for dispensing practical wisdom and moral truth that otherwise might be lost in an academic venue. When we read or hear a story we find ourselves feeling for the characters through their speech and thoughts. We often identify and empathize with their fears, hopes, dreams and expectations. Most importantly, from their successes and failures we can learn lessons for life. Stories have the power to change us—and indeed they do!

The *Let's Ask Auntie Anne* series consist of five stories and five pertinent parenting themes. Each story is embedded with practical advice that will guide the reader to greater understanding of the complexities of childrearing and hopefully serve as a friend to motivate positive change.

Finally, the series was designed for individual or group study. The questions at the end of each book both remind and highlight the significant principles of the lessons taught. Whether you read for your own pleasure or share with a community of friends, we know you will benefit from a trip to Auntie Anne's kitchen and her treasury of parenting knowledge. Enjoy.

Gary and Anne Marie Ezzo
Mt. Pleasant, South Carolina
August 2004

Meet the Real Auntie Anne

Eleanor Roosevelt insightfully concluded that "Beautiful young people are accidents of nature, but beautiful old people are works of art." The main character in this book is, as the former First Lady described, a beautiful work of art, fashioned by the colors of life.

Auntie Anne is not a fictional character. She was born in Boston, Massachusetts, on March 24, 1914. Her life, while not as glamorous as Eleanor Roosevelt's has indeed been greatly influential. With an earthly common sense that often eludes others and a sense of humor that never fails, this amazing woman of ninety-plus years continues to endear herself to friend and stranger.

Each book in this series is as much a tribute to a beautiful life as it is a parenting resource filled with timeless wisdom and practical application. In each story (just as in real life), Auntie Anne is cheerfully spry, physically capable, neither failing in sight nor mind. A philosopher of sorts, and like those of her day, her interest extends into all areas. The mind, she believes, has no limits but those we choose to give it, and hungry minds, whether of children or the elderly, need the food of useful knowledge—*daily*.

In real life, the children who called Auntie Anne "Mom" were children of aristocrats, professors, and other notables from the fair cities up North. No, they were not her children by birth, but by design. As a Boston nanny, she loved them as a mother loves her own. She would weave buttercup crowns and sing treasured melodies. She cooked extravagantly and lusciously—spices and herbs, warm buttered bread, and crusty apple cobbler baked to a beautiful brown hue. Reading followed mealtimes routinely. Each of the children under Auntie Anne's care were taught to love books. She took them through literary adventures with Dickens, Poe, T. S. Eliot, Tolkien, Hemingway, Bunyan, and more.

The beautiful, historical City of Charleston, South Carolina, frames the backdrop for the series. Auntie Anne draws her parenting lessons from the city's rich history and the daily life of people living on or near the Carolina saltwater marshes. Charleston's glorious past from the Colonial period through the American Revolution, the Civil War, and into the present day and the beauty of its perfectly maintained historical district, cobblestone streets and waterfront parks are all woven into Auntie Anne's lessons.

From her kitchen window she overlooks the wide green marsh and the blue waters of the Wando River in the lovely neighboring town of Mt. Pleasant. The descriptions of places, scenes, and the anecdotal stories in each book are factual. Apart from Auntie Anne, the characters in our stories are fictional but their needs accurately reflect the many common concerns and challenges for today's parents. The authors speak through Auntie Anne's life story to satisfy the needs of each inquiring couple.

Come and enjoy. Put on your slippers, find a quiet nook, and benefit from a trip to RiverTowne, and Auntie Anne's kitchen. If you can picture a home by the water, a flowered paradise of sorts, with a vista of blue skies and green marshes, where birds and butterflies fill the air and the scent of ocean mingles with a Carolina morning, then you have successfully imagined Auntie Anne's home at the water's edge. Here you will find a friend, one who connects for a new generation of parents the *descriptive*—the way it was and the way it is—with the *prescriptive*—the way it should be.

Meet the Carriage Couples

Ít all goes back to Missy. Of course, she could not have known the train of events to spin out of her spunky fondness for hopping in cars not her own. Nor does she own a car. This Missy, oh beg your pardon, is a dog. A fluffy white pedigree peek-a-poo with a Rottweiler complex and a James Cagney smile.

When she hopped in the car of Geoff and Ginger Portier on that Saturday night so long ago, no one could have imagined the chain of events that would eventually lead five couples on a journey of discovery about themselves and their parenting. In one of life's paradoxical moments, the beginning often becomes clearer in light of the end and so it is with our story.

It was through the strange encounter with Missy, that the Portiers first met Auntie Anne. (Narrative is found in Book Five.) It only took one delightful Sunday afternoon sipping sweet tea and playing a game of Scrabble for Geoff and Ginger to discover the treasury of Auntie Anne's knowledge.

Auntie Anne is more than a good person at heart and

a wonderful chef in the kitchen, she is also a wise sage, a woman gifted in thought with a plentiful supply of grace and charm. All of this accented by a marvelous wit. Yes, a refreshing wit that compliments her clean heart and noble mind.

In a time of desperation and perplexing challenges our dear Auntie Anne brings much needed correction and aid to Geoff and Ginger's parenting. From that experience, others would come to know of this woman's marvelous gifts.

The following Spring five couples crowded together on the padded seats of an old wooden carriage harnessed to two brown mules named Knick and Knack. Two-week-old chicks circled underfoot, pecking eagerly at feed dropped from the mules' grain bags.

A minute later, the driver shook the reins and called, "Eeyuup." Twenty-two-hundred pounds of muscle lunged forward as chicks scattered in every direction. The carriage swayed out of the big red barn to the rhythm of creaking wood and clopping hoofs. Another tour of historical Charleston, South Carolina had begun with a promise of a blessing.

Coincidence or destiny? It mattered little. It was just one of those odd occurrences in life. Five couples, strangers to each other, meet randomly on a bright and sunny Carolina morning and everything clicked. A few minutes into the carriage ride and the couples were already talking about their children left at home. School pictures traveled up and down the rows greeted by smiles and nodding heads. The tour of Charleston's historical district took just over an hour and by the time the carriage returned to the big red barn, the couples were talking like old friends. Charleston has a way of doing that, making everyone feel like family.

It was Geoff and Ginger Portier who brought up the idea of lunch. Eyes met and heads nodded and before long, five couples set out to enjoy one of the Charleston's delightful bistros. Settling in with iced chai, and a few diet cokes, the couples talked about the high points of the tour before the topic turned once again to their children, parenting and life on the home-front.

It was than that Geoff and Ginger directed the conversation by sharing what they considered to be one of Charleston's best kept secrets.

"Her name," Geoff said, "is Auntie Anne and she can change your life. Her thoughts are relevant, her searching mind insightful, and her understanding of the human heart runs deep and wide."

"She is a refreshing change from all the parenting experts I've read lately," Ginger added, "and her wise counsel is gentle and affective."

"If you need help with parenting, and find yourself frustrated with your other options, pay a little visit to Auntie Anne. There are only two things required," Geoff went on to say. "First, play a game of Scrabble with the dear woman and second, talk nice to her little dog Missy."

Geoff and Ginger continued with their celebration of Auntie Anne, sharing about that memorable Sunday afternoon months ago. The contagious energy of their enthusiasm was food for the weary soul and put hope and expectancy in the hearts of their new friends. Now peeked with curiosity and a secret longing for assistance, each couple over time would find their way to the big green house near the water's edge. The place where Auntie Anne calls home.

There are five couples and five unique parenting challenges. Listen in as Auntie Anne satisfies each inquiry with relevant and practical "rubber meets the road" advice.

In Book One, Mac and Vicki Lake can not figure out why their children act as if they are not loved. Mom and Dad are missing something so basic that even the simple phrase "I love you" falls short of its intended meaning. How well did Auntie Anne help them? You decide after reading *How to Raise a Loving Child*.

In Book Two, meet Bill and Elaine Lewis. Who doesn't know at least one family facing the frustration of irresponsible children? Messy rooms, wet towels on the floor, and unfinished homework are just the beginning. Join Bill and Elaine as they go with Auntie Anne on a journey to the heart of *How to Raise a Responsible Child*.

In Book Three, little do Rick and Lela Harvey know that a lack of security is the root of their children's behavioral problems. Nervous, irritable children acting out at school in seemingly uncontrollable ways are a dead giveaway. Auntie Anne has a plan for this home. Find out what and *who* needs to change in *How to Raise a Secure Child*.

In Book Four, Clarke and Mia Forden seek out Auntie Anne's advice on building trusting relationships. For Clarke and Mia, the pace of today's family is troubling. How will fathers capture the hearts of their children with so little time? Find out what they wished they had learned a dozen years earlier in *How to Raise a Trusting Child.*

In Book Five, Geoff and Ginger Portier tell their story of how Auntie Anne taught them how to make virtues and values real in the lives of their children. What will it take to create a love for moral beauty within the heart of their children? Auntie Anne provides solid answers in *How to Raise a Moral Child.*

Introduction

Mac and Vicki lead busy, successful lives while trying to raise five children. Their days were so busy fulfilling multiple obligations and meeting optional goals that they missed some major gaps in their parenting. Oh yes, they knew they had some problems, but what they didn't recognize was just how starved their children were for love.

Becka, soon to be thirteen, seems like the model first-born child and is very popular at school. The twins, Jack and Jillian, are eleven. Jack is at the top of his class and a master musician to boot, and Jillian is active in clubs, a real volunteer. R. J. (short for Robert Joseph) is nine and is a load of fun to be with, while six-year-old Emily, the baby, has all the adorable traits of her siblings mixed together.

Still, Mom and Dad are troubled. Becka always seems to have to be the center of attention, and while Jack dots every *i* and crosses every *t,* he doesn't handle competition well. They suspect that Jillian's few close friends like her because of what she gives them, not for

Jillian herself. R.J. appears stable, but he goes ballistic whenever Mom and Dad try to enjoy some time by themselves, and little Emily seems to need constant approval and praise.

With the encouragement of the other carriage couples, Vicki and Mac have decided to pay a visit to Auntie Anne in the hope that she can help them uncover the mystery behind their children's troubling behavior. On this warm spring day, Auntie Anne is ready and waiting. So far this morning, she has finished a green and yellow quilt, watered her flowers, and played toss with Missy. Now she's eager to meet some new friends.

~ On The Way ~

Vicki added a dab of gloss to her already cherry red lips and closed her compact. "There," she said, "the finishing touch before the big meeting." The bright June sun made the Carolina morning just like the song said—nothing could be finer.

Mac turned off Highway 41 onto RiverTowne Parkway and began searching for the lone stop sign described in their scribbled directions. Here and there large sprawling oaks draped with Spanish moss enhanced the feeling that they were in a different time, and perhaps in a different world. Vicki mumbled her favorite Judy Garland line: "Toto, I don't think we're in Kansas anymore."

Mac just smiled. He heard that line a hundred times before.

They drove past homes with well-manicured lawns, black hurricane shutters, and flower-accented porches where white rocking chairs beckoned visitors to come, sit, and rest. Beyond the houses lay the village green, bordered by two ponds shimmering blue. Irregular circles of lily pads reflected drops of dew sparkling in the morning sun and crowned by white lilies with yellow pistil blooms. At the edge of the villages green stood a tidy brick building with a single sign that read RIVERTOWNE POSTAL CENTER.

"Look, Mac," Vicki said, pointing out the window. "They have their own little post office here. Isn't that quaint? It gives you that community feel."

Mac turned his head toward the picturesque structure and then surveyed both sides of the street. "Yeah, it looks like there aren't any mailboxes. That could get annoying, don't you think, Vic? You know, coming all this way just to get your mail."

Vicki couldn't help wondering what it would be like to live in a place that required constant contact with a community of neighbors. She thought about this mysterious and enchanting world of Auntie Anne's. So many smiling faces and friendly waves. Though she was drawn to romanticism, Vicki knew that living so connected with others would leave her vulnerable.

They slowly drove past a second line of houses, each with Victorian accents and sweeping verandas. Large hanging baskets of flowers graced the porches adding a colorful ambiance to the restful atmosphere. White picket fences with yellow, red and blue lantana mixed with Mexican heather poked bright purple stems through the slates making a fitting border to a scene that looked like a Thomas Kinkade painting. Butterflies drifted in and out through the patches of light between the shade of the trees, and the peace and beauty of a spring morning rested on the day like a benediction.

At the stop sign they paused to check the street names and numbers. Mac was in no hurry to reach their destination. In fact, he wasn't even sure he wanted to meet with Auntie Anne at all. Getting help with parenting, from a stranger no less, plucked at a chord of his pride that he preferred left unplayed.

After all, things weren't that bad at home. Life was even pretty good, and good enough should be left alone. That was his approach to family problems. For Mac, this visit to Auntie Anne was more about fitting in with the carriage couples than getting help with parenting.

"Look there, Mac." His eyes followed Vicki's pointing finger to a red brick footpath leading to a large white gazebo on the village common.

"Another meeting spot for the neighborhood, I'll bet," Vicki said.

The scene transported them to another time and place, where ice cream socials and four-part harmony of barbershop quartets joined the sounds of children's laughter and clapping hands during weekly concerts. "This place isn't real, Vic," Mac said, his gaze now galvanized on the scene.

Mac turned left, and Vicki spotted the green home belonging to Auntie Anne. "This is it," she said. Mac pulled into the driveway and parked the car.

"Isn't this something!" Vicki said slightly overwhelmed. The large, airy home, with its flower-laden steps leading to the porch and four rocking chairs, was reminiscent of a way of life not yet finished nor forgotten.

Mac got out of the car and stretched, waiting for Vicki to join him.

"Shall we?" Vicki said, turning to Mac. He nodded and they ascended the stairs. Taking a deep breath, he pushed the doorbell and waited. No sound could be heard except from the back of the house where children's laugher and a dog barking caught Mac's attention.

"Let's check out back Vic." Mac turned and headed back down the steps, forcing Vicki to hustle to keep up. Flip-flopping his car keys over and under his hand, he moved around the corner to the side gate. Then, just beyond the third palmetto tree, they saw her. Unmistakably, it was Auntie Anne.

~ The Greeting ~

Two women stood chatting over a waist-high fence in the shadow of a tall palm. One was undoubtedly Auntie Anne; the other was a lovely African-American woman nearly thirty years her junior. Behind them three young children were chasing a leaping green creature, no doubt of froglike origin, capable of amazing gravity-defying maneuvers.

Auntie Anne turned to the newcomers and waved. Mac and Vicki waved back, smiling as Auntie Anne approached the gate.

"Good morning folks, come in. The latch is right there." Auntie Anne said pointing toward the gate.

Mac reached down to release the lever holding the gate closed.

"We're just watching Barbara's grandchildren carry out a science project. Did you know that tree frogs have suction cups attached to their feet? Talk about a tough life."

Mac found himself smiling. "You must be the one and only Auntie Anne," he said.

"That's me, and you must be Mr. Mac and Miss Vicki. Mr. Geoff said you were the punctual type, and sure enough, you're right on time."

Off to the side a white dog was poking her wild-haired head between two picket posts, watching the commotion next door and wagging her tail at top speed as if to propel her furry little body into the action. "That must be Missy," Vicki said, extending her hand to greet Auntie Anne.

Auntie Anne met Vicki's extended hand with her own. "Yes, that's her all right. Now I want you to meet Barbara." To Mac's surprise, Auntie Anne suddenly took hold of his left arm like a bride holding her groom and gently nudged him toward the fence.

The two strolled together over the freshly mowed lawn, breathing in the scent of white jasmine. Mac felt strange. Somehow Auntie Anne's gesture of taking his arm had opened a book and Mac tried to interpret the message filling his heart. He felt immediately accepted by her. Her touch communicated a type of trust, a sense of approval. There was something about this woman that was strong, yet gently persuasive. Mac found himself quickly getting caught up in Auntie Anne's world and that was okay with him.

"Barbara, this is Mac and Vicki, friends of Geoff and Ginger. You know, the folks who moved up to Columbia last year?"

"I'm pleased to meet you both," Barbara said.

"Barb's a native Charlestonian. She moved back a couple years ago after twenty-eight years up in Baltimore."

"What brought you back?" Mac inquired.

"When my husband passed on seven years ago, I knew it was time." A sad note crept into her voice at the mention of her husband. "My family's here, so this is the right place for me."

"Not a bad spot to come home to," Vicki commented, glancing at the large riverfront home and then out to the marshes and the Wando River beyond. "It's nice to meet you Barbara."

"Well Barb, you have fun with those grandkids. The three of us have some visiting to do inside." Still holding Mac's arm, Auntie Anne strolled toward the house, waving good-bye over her shoulder with her free hand.

Mac, who had determined not to let his guard down with this woman, was quickly slipping. His first impression was one of strength and gentleness. Not that she had performed any feats before his eyes. Yet, there was something in her countenance, a way that commended gentle persuasion. As it is said, nothing is as strong as gentleness and nothing is as gentle as real strength. Here a woman of nine decades exudes both.

The back entrance to Auntie Anne's home was as beautifully adorned as the front. Mac and Vicki admired the pink and purple petunias growing in the shadows of the Carolina jasmine both waiting patiently for the afternoon sun. A playful breath of sea air tickled their noses as they climbed the stairs.

~ Beyond the Marsh ~

"Come in out of the heat," Auntie Anne said leading the way to the back entrance. Mac and Vicki followed Auntie Anne into the great room. Though the room was large, it felt cozy and inviting. Auntie Anne had filled its shelves with mementos and heirlooms that would laugh and sing if they could. The focal point of the room were six large window's that framed a view of the lush green marsh and the deep blue water beyond.

A movement outside caught Vicki's eye. "Look Mac at the bird stalking," she said pointing toward the marsh. "Auntie Anne, is that an egret? It's so…."

Her words trailed off at the odd rhythmic sound of *ca-chug, ca-chug, ca-chug*. Looking downriver, she spotted the source of the noise. "Oh, Mac, it's a tugboat pushing a huge barge, and it's going to cruise right past this window. It's so close!"

"Auntie Anne, this is something," Vicki said excitedly. "Do a lot of boats pass by every day?"

"We get all kinds here. I see big ones like this and small ones no bigger than a bathtub. The one thing they all have in common is that they can sink." She turned and headed to the kitchen, inviting her visitors to follow.

"Sounds like you've seen them all," Vicki said, moving toward the kitchen nook. "Which do you like best?"

Auntie Anne turned to look again at the dark vessel gliding through the water.

"I enjoy them all. It's the same on the river as it is in life—variety is what makes it all beautiful."

Excusing herself, Auntie Anne stepped out on the back porch, and clapped her hands twice. Seconds later, Missy bounded up the stairs, wagging her tail as if she was greeting an old friend. "Come on in, Missy. We've got company." Missy followed Auntie Anne into the kitchen and made a few sniffing laps around the chairs before stretching herself out on the cool hardwood floor.

"Auntie Anne, it's such a treat to finally meet you." Vicki said. "We've heard so much about you from Geoff and Ginger."

"Well, I'm glad to meet any friend of Mr. Geoff and Miss Ginger. They're a sweet couple. I miss seeing them, now that they're up in Columbia. Oh well. How about something cool to drink this morning? I have a pitcher of sweet tea over on the counter there near the fridge and a tray. Miss Vicki would you mind pouring the glasses for us and bringing them to the table?"

Vicki nodded and offered a gentle "Okay." She moved toward the pitcher and began pouring the caramel-colored tea into three tall frosted glasses. Auntie Anne had disappeared out to the back porch off the kitchen. She returned holding up three deep green leaves, each slightly larger than a guitar pick. "Mint. It grows nearly wild in this climate," she said. She rinsed each leaf carefully before dropping it into each glass. The three sat at Auntie Anne's table sharing an exquisite view of the lush green marsh and the river beyond.

"Well then, Mac, tell me about the children. How old are they?"

"We have five children. There's Becka. She'll be thirteen next week. Jack and Jillian are eleven-year-old twins, R. J. is nine, and Emily just turned five. No, six."

"Becka is at the top of her class," Vicki added, "and Jack's an accomplished pianist and saxophone player. Jill excels at sports and also plays the violin. R.J., well he loves everything, except when we leave for a weekend. Emily is a little bit of all of them." Vicki realized she was rambling and stopped.

"That's a bunch of emotional tanks needing to be filled with love every day," Auntie Anne said.

Vicki suspended her glass halfway to her lips, and it hung there a moment before completing its trip to her mouth. Mac fixed his eyes on Auntie Anne, wondering what she was getting at.

"We do love our children, Auntie Anne. I mean we do all we can. Well, we try every day. Really. We teach them right from wrong, we take them to different places to learn about the world, and we make sure they have everything they need." Vicki looked at Mac as if for permission to continue. Turning back to Auntie Anne Vicki continued. "But the truth is, they just don't seem to respond to the love we offer. There's almost a distance between us and the children." Tears began to fill her eyes. "It seems like we're just seven people existing under

31

the same roof. I don't know why I'm telling you all of this…. I'm sorry to be going on and on."

"I'm glad you feel comfortable enough to share the burden of your heart with me Vicki," Auntie Anne said encouragingly.

"We love all of our children very much, Auntie Anne," Mac added, "and we have high hopes for each of them. But sometimes it seems we're not connecting with them, because they just don't behave like children who are loved. I can't say it any clearer than that." He shook his head, frustrated by his inability to put the problem into words.

Auntie Anne smiled. "Ahh, love is tricky stuff," she said adding a lighter air to what felt like a discouraging moment. "Love is something we give through the things we do and say, but it is tricky business," she said slowly nodding with the rhythm of her words.

"Tricky stuff, Auntie Anne?" Mac asked.

"Oh yes! It can be quite challenging trying to figure out which child gets what and when and how much."

"Do you mean that there's just so much love to be divided up and that each child gets a little portion for the day?" Mac asked.

Auntie Anne smiled at Mac and slowly shook her head. "It's not about giving your children portions of your love, but about filling up their love tanks every day. The tricky part is to know what to serve each child. What makes Becka grow? And what do you serve Jack or Jillian, and R. J. and Emily?"

Wide-eyed, Vicki and Mac looked at each other. They wanted more. They needed more.

"Please go on, Auntie Anne," Vicki said. "What do you mean about serving them different meals?"

"Well, you, me, Miss Barbara, and those dear children of yours all need love, but we don't all sense the power of love in the same way. That's why there are problems." Auntie Anne paused for a moment. She took her napkin and wiped the excess moisture off the side of her glass. "Let me give you a little history about the start up of old Charles Towne."

~ I Don't Understand You ~

"Few people realize that the original Charles Towne settlement of 1670 was the work of eight English Lord Proprietors seeking financial gain in the new lands, and *not* folks seeking religious freedom. Oh, many came for religious freedom, but unlike most settlements up north, the Charles Towne colony was a straightforward entrepreneurial venture. Free enterprise flourished, and the colony became profitable. Well, you can imagine that when word got back to Old Europe that money could be made in the Americas' southern colony, people began to flock here from all over. English, Germans, Swedes, and French Huguenots all became part of a mix. The slave trade brought people from many different African villages and dialects. They were all met by the local Indian tribes, the Kiawah, Sewee, Santee, and Wandoes."

Auntie Anne gave a long pause. "Now think about all the confusion there must have been with so many languages being spoken in one place."

"If you wanted to survive here," Mac said, "I think you would have needed to learn to speak more than one language."

"I would think so, too" Auntie Anne continued. "So many languages and everyone tends to speak their native tongue to everyone they meet. Confusion! Yes, there was much potential for confusion and mis-understanding when it came to bartering, trading and everyday living."

"I've never really thought about those types of chal-lenges faced by the first settlers," Vicki said, "but what you say does make sense."

"Just think about it. If you grew up speaking only English, that would work just fine in a home where only English was spoken, but it might not work so well if you visited the French Huguenot church for Sunday service."

"Oh, we saw that church on our tour of Charleston with the carriage couples. It's just down from St. Phillips. Remember Mac?" Vicki said.

"Yes, and I think they still conduct a service or two in French," Mac added.

Auntie Anne nodded her agreement. "Think what would happen if you went to church there and didn't speak French. You wouldn't know what was going on and you would feel like an outsider. You simply can't build a close relationship with people when you don't speak their language."

Vicki leaned forward, resting her elbows on the table, and cupped her chin in her hands. She looked at Mac and back to Auntie Anne. "I'm sorry," she said. "This is fascinating, but what does this have to do with our five children?"

Mac wasn't sure either, but he was content keeping that to himself. "Auntie Anne, can you help Vicki better understand your point here?"

Vicki shot a smile over at Mac, snapping her finger against his arm.

"Well, let's find out," Auntie said with a smile. She

got up and walked to an old painted cupboard. "This is where I keep the Scrabble board. Maybe we can discuss all of this over a game."

"Mac, you help Auntie Anne get the board set up, and I'm going to get my notepad out." Vicki reached into her purse for a pen and a new steno pad.

"Vicki," Mac whispered, "What are you doing?"

Vicki lowered her voice but enunciated each word clearly as if she were practicing ventriloquism. She looked up, "Mac," she said in a low voice, "Ginger said that this is the time to take notes. This is when Auntie Anne gives us the answers."

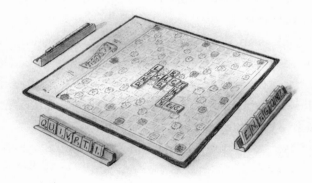

Auntie Anne returned with the Scrabble game and set the well-worn cardboard box on the table. With the cover removed everyone busied themselves setting up the board, trays, and pulling letters from the dark blue velvet bag. Mac watched wide-eyed as Auntie Anne shuffled her letters in full concentration.

Vicki began the game with the word *swing*—a simple word full of sweet imagery. Auntie Anne contributed *agape,* a Greek word for love. Mac came up with *slake*.

"Mac," Vicki said , "Shouldn't that be *snake*?"

"No, my dear wife, it's *slake*."

"I've never heard of *slake*. Is that a word, Auntie Anne?"

"Oh yes, it is. It means to quench a thirst. It's a good word."

Mac sat back in his chair, smiling, arms folded. "Auntie Anne," he said. "You know a lot of words. Do you speak any other languages?" Mac asked hoping to return to the history lesson.

"Well, I guess that depends on which languages you're referring to." Auntie Anne turned the question back to Mac.

While he was thinking about it, Vicki added *pretty* to the board and reached into the velvet bag for more letters. Vicki's hand paused in the bag, "Mac, where are you? Auntie Anne was talking to you."

"No, I'm here. I was just processing her comment about the types of languages. Have I missed something,

Auntie Anne?" Mac asked. "I mean with this language stuff. What kind of languages are you referring to?"

Auntie Anne lifted her head from her tray of letters. "I do speak Italian and bits of Portuguese and Spanish, and of course, I'm *fluent* in puppy language. But over the years I've learned other important languages—not the ones spoken by the tongue, but by the heart. That's the honey that keeps the bees home."

Okay, we're going someplace with this, Mac thought. "Vicki, get ready to take some notes," Mac said light-heartedly.

"Mac, what if everyone in your family spoke a different language? What if Becka spoke French, Jack spoke Russian, Jillian spoke Swahili, R. J. spoke Cantonese, and Emily spoke Spanish? How difficult would it be for all of you to connect, especially if the only language you and Vicki spoke was English? How much confusion would there be in your home?"

"Oh, Auntie Anne," Vicki interrupted, "we have some of that confusion in our house right now. And I for one get so frustrated because it seems like everything I say or do gets misinterpreted by my five… no, six darlings" Vicki pointed her thumb in Mac's direction.

Auntie Anne gave Vicki an understanding nod and continued. "There are problems of mistrust and feelings of disappointment and isolation that come when a love message is misinterpreted. You thought you were saying one thing, and they interpreted your words or actions to mean something different."

"Exactly. It's like we're not speaking their primary love language." Mac paused after hearing his own words. He suddenly realized that he may have said something profound.

"Are we having an *aha* moment here?" Vicki asked. She wasn't sure she could connect all the dots, but somehow she knew that Auntie Anne would do it for her.

The pleasurable scent of jasmine drifted in through the screened porch, finding its way to the kitchen. A couple of bees bumped the porch screen, catching Auntie Anne's eye. Auntie Anne slowly placed her letters on the board, intersecting Vicki's last word. "There, *honey*." She looked in Vicki's direction. "Bees are interesting creatures, always busy," Auntie Anne began as she lifted a finger and pointed at the porch screen.

Mac and Vicki glanced over. "They're always searching for sweet nectar, flying into every flower and bloom they can find. From the high mountains to the low deserts, they seek out the sweetness. Busy creatures indeed, make no mistake about it. But there are no fools in the animal kingdom. Even a bee won't gather nectar if there's a supply of ready-made honey right outside the hive. Bees will feed on that one source, bring it back to the hive, and look no further."

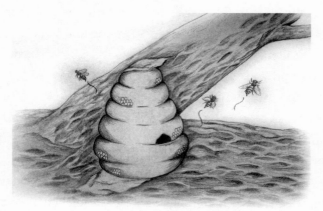

Auntie Anne paused to allow Vicki and Mac's thoughts time to catch up to her imagery. "Your children are like those bees," she continued. "They'll look high and low for the sweet nectar that satisfies them. But if a supply of honey is already present, they'll feed from that one source and wander no more."

"Auntie Anne," Vicki said softly, eyes wide with wonder. "How is it possible that you know all these things?"

"Well, after nine decades you start to decode many of life's riddles." She paused and grinned. "Watching

Discovery Channel is a big help, too."

Mac gave a small snorty laugh. Vicki patted Auntie Anne's hand.

"Auntie Anne, how can Vicki and I provide the sweet honey that will keep our children close to us? That is your point, isn't it?"

"Oh, I can tell you how to do that. You must learn the sweet languages of love and speak them to your children."

"You mean," Vicki paused to collect her thoughts, "we should speak nicely to them, in a soft and gentle Mommy-adores-you kind of voice?" She gave her best impression of a nice-mommy tone with her last words, earning soft applause from Mac.

"Well, soft words *are* very important for children to hear and the Good Book says a soft word turns away anger. But I'm talking about the sweet languages that touch the emotions and make people feel truly loved. Every child experiences love differently and they communicate it differently. We all speak different emotional languages. It's part of our God-given uniqueness."

Mac took a deep breath. "So you're saying that all children have an emotional love language that's unique to them—different from their brothers or sisters?"

"Not just different from their brothers and sisters,

Mac, but often different from their parents. You say 'I love you' in English, but Becka says it in French and Vicki speaks Portuguese. Can you see the potential for confusion? We can work on your linguistic skills this morning if you'd like. But first, whose turn is it?"

"Is it yours, Vicki?"

"No, Mac, I think it's your turn. Do you have a word?"

"Sure, it's *overwhelmed*." He grinned. "I just don't have enough letters. For now, I'll stick with *slow*." He placed the tiles on the board, intersecting *honey*.

"That's a fine word," Auntie Anne said. "Sometimes slow is good. Moving too fast isn't always the best way to get somewhere. Let's go slow with this love stuff."

"We're ready," Mac said eagerly. Vicki nodded with enthusiasm.

~ Saying I Love You With Quality Time ~

"Did you kids see the rockers this morning on your drive in?" Auntie Anne asked.

For a moment, Vicki's face had a bemused expression. Then she said, "Oh, you mean the rocking chairs! At first, I thought you meant rockers, like kids who listen to rock and roll! Yes, we saw them."

"They were very inviting," Mac said. "I could envision Vicki and myself sitting in them, sipping sweet tea, and sharing a relaxing moment at the end of the day. Who sells them? We could use a couple for our back deck."

"You can get them most anywhere," Auntie Anne answered. "No matter where you get them, they all come with my personal guarantee." Her nimble fingers pushed each letter of the word *enjoy* into place.

"Your personal guarantee?"

"Yes sir," she said. "If you follow the instructions for use, that is."

"Ahh, the instructions," Vicki said. "That's where they get you. Somewhere in the small print."

"And just what is it about the rockers that you guarantee?" Mac asked with a grin. "That they'll last a lifetime if you don't sit on them?" He placed *yodels* on the board for a double-word score.

"No, Mr. Mac, just the opposite. You see, most folks want what a rocker promises. It is a symbol of warmth and sharing of an era when people still took time to be together, when conversation was cherished and not considered a form of amusement. People buy the rockers and then forget what they're for. So they lose the lifetime guarantee."

"And what is that guarantee, Auntie Anne?"

"The guarantee is that if you spend time rocking with someone you care about, you will send a love gift wrapped in quality time. Giving someone quality time is a way of saying 'I love you.' Sitting and rocking reconnects souls. But to reap the rewards, you have to take the time to sit and rock and share." Otherwise, the rocker is just a symbol of what is possible but not the reality that many hope for."

"Symbols! I guess our lives are full of symbols we substitute for reality." Mac said as a self-evaluating statement. "The rocking chairs are like a two edged sword. On one side, it's a reminder of a blessing we could have, on the other side, the silent reminder of what we have been missing."

Vicki squeezed her eyebrows together. "I'm sorry," she said, "but I'm not tracking with you. What are you two talking about?"

"We're talking about things in our life that are only symbols of things we want to be real," Mac said. "In time the symbols become substitutes for what we're really hoping for. It's like those rocking chairs on the porches, Vick. They look real pretty, but they're empty. That's the point Auntie Anne is making."

"Yes Mac, that is! You have to set aside time to enjoy

the rocker in order to get the benefits. Sitting in them makes beautiful memories that carry you into the future. Twenty years down the road, you'll have something special."

"Like a worn-out rocker." Mac laughed.

"Well, I think you kids get the point. It isn't the rocker; it's the quality time a rocker affords. It could be spending time on your couch, in your backyard, at a park—these are the rocking chairs of life that children remember. Quality time may be the primary language of love for one of your children."

"Auntie Anne," Vicki started as she turned her head in Mac's direction and then back to Auntie Anne's. "Becka is our quality time child. She loves it when we spend time with her. In fact, she comes alive when we give her our undivided attention. Maybe that is why she loves it when we sit beside her and help with her homework. She is the most agreeable and pleasant child to be with when we spend time with her."

"That's true, Vick," Mac said. "Becka is the most delightful child to be with. The only time her behavior is troublesome is when we fail to give her quality attention on a regular basis."

Vicki acknowledged Mac's realization with a nod while contemplating the reality his words. She slowly rearranged her letters on her tray but her heart was elsewhere. A moment later she placed *linger* on the board. Vickie was lost now trying to remember the last time she and Becka had spent time talking about something other than schoolwork or lines for a play or how to eat like a lady. Quality time was a language she needed to learn to speak, for Becka's sake.

"I'm getting it Auntie Anne," Mac said. "If there's no honey at home, the bee must look elsewhere for nectar to make it. And for Becka, honey is quality time."

"Sticky stuff, this search for honey," Vicki said looking at Mac.

Auntie Anne agreed. "You are both right. Parents must stay mindful that just as all children are different, so are their honey needs."

~ Saying I Love You with Touch ~

Auntie Anne reached forward adding the word *contact* to the board, and then suddenly stood up and briskly retrieved the pitcher of tea and returned to the table. Mac studied his own letters while Auntie Anne refreshed all the drinks. He knew he was within striking range of Auntie Anne's score, and his competitive nature kicked in. "Okay, here I go," he said. He placed *recess* on the board.

Vicki added *rule,* not at all concerned about her trailing points.

Without a moment's hesitation, Auntie Anne laid down *close* for a triple-word score.

All of a sudden a sound from the river commanded everyone's attention.

Vicki looked up and then tapped Mac's arm. "Look at that boat coming down the river."

"What kind of boat is that with all the nets on the side?" Mac asked.

"That's a shrimp boat. There are lots of them around here. This is Bubba Gump country. Beautiful, isn't it?"

Missy jumped up from the padded pillow in the

blue-gray puppy travel bag that served as her kennel and joined the staring threesome. She put her front paws on the windowsill, and her eyes followed everyone's gaze to the water. The boat did not intrigue her, but the sea-gulls had potential gaming interest.

"Oh, this is wonderful. Watch carefully now," Auntie Anne said as she pointed to the marsh grass. "Nature is about to speak to us."

Mac and Vicki exchanged smiles and returned their gaze to the river, not exactly sure what to look for.

"Calming, isn't it, Mac?" Vicki said, her eyes fixed on the trawler's smooth, steady motion as its bow broke the surface of the water.

"Here it comes," Auntie Anne said. "Watch how the marsh greets the wake."

As the wake of the trawler spread through the fifty yards of marsh, the grasses began to bob their heads in rhythmic unison. Back and forth the stems danced as the marsh held the water and then released it. Soon the entire marsh was alive with movement.

"Notice how the marsh grass offers no resistance to the wave, but rather welcomes its embrace? Morning till night, each blade waits patiently for the caress of the water. Together, the wake and the grass create something beautiful that neither would experience without the other."

Moved by Auntie Anne's poetic description, Mac contemplated the supple limbs of grassy plant life along the river's sidelines, stretching out to greet the sparkling blue water's edge.

"There's power in the touch," Auntie Anne continued. "It makes those who receive it feel accepted, and they long relive the moment in their memories. We were all created with millions of touch receptors so we could give and receive sensations of love, comfort, and security."

Vicki recalled the long embraces she had shared with each of her children before she and Mac left home.

"For some children," Auntie Anne continued, "physical touch and closeness communicates the message 'I love you.' All children need hugs, but for some, physical touch and closeness is the primary way they know that they're loved, secure, and special. You'll recognize kids like this. They're always ready to give a hug, or receive an embrace, just as the green grasses receive the water's loving touch. They want to be close to you, sit on your lap, or next to you at church, or hold your hand. Do you know anyone like that?"

Immediately and in unison, Mac and Vicki said, "R.J."

"That fits him to a T," Vicki said. "He always wants to hold hands or climb into our laps during a movie. Oh my, how many times did I think he was just a squirmy kid? And all the time he was seeking love from me through physical touch. Mac, you're like that too."

"A squirmy kid?"

"No, like R. J., with his need for physical touch."

Mac sat back in his chair, arms folded, thinking about the reassuring feeling he had earlier that morning when Auntie Anne had taken his arm and began strolling with him. "I do understand how R. J. feels," he said. "That… that feeling of unconditional acceptance and love that comes from closeness and touch."

Auntie Anne nodded looking directly into Mac's eyes. "Of course Mac you understand the feeling. Doesn't a cheetah recognize the tracks of another cheetah?"

Mac and Vicki watched the deep green marsh grass catch the last embrace of the boat's wake. Mac reflected on the nighttime rituals back home. Every night it was the same thing. He thought R. J. was trying to sneak in more time with his "another hug" routine, rather than going to bed, content like the other kids. "It's not that he always wants to be with us," Mac said, "but when he is with us, he always likes being close."

"How do fathers miss these things?" he mumbled

to himself with the sad realization that he was guilty of missing the obvious in R.J.'s life. They both silently yearned to return home, right now, and hold their little guy.

Auntie Anne gave them time to reflect. Then she said, "Okay, let's see.... Mr. Mac, I think it's your turn."

~ Saying I Love You Through Gift-giving ~

Mac had just added *words* to the board when the doorbell rang. Aroused from a deep sleep, Missy stretched and trotted to the front door, tail wagging.

Auntie Anne pushed her chair back and rose. "Excuse me," she said with a slight nod. Looking past the dining room out to the front piazza she saw a little girl. Auntie Anne smiled. "It's my Kara."

Swinging the door open with one hand, Auntie Anne greeted the visitor. "Kara, come in. What do you have there?"

Kara gave Auntie Anne a big smile and handed her a small basket. Peeking under the red and white checkered cloth, Auntie Anne's face lit up. "Oh, Kara, are these what I think they are?"

Kara beamed.

"Come into the kitchen Kara, I want you to meet

51

some friends."

The ten-year-old followed Auntie Anne. On the way, she reached down to scoop up Missy for a cuddle. Auntie Anne introduced Kara to Mac and Vicki, and they exchanged greetings. Then Auntie Anne unveiled cookies bursting with chocolate chips and nuts. "You've made some fine cookies here, Kara," she said. "Nothing says lovin' like something from the oven, and these cookies look '*mm-mmm*' good."

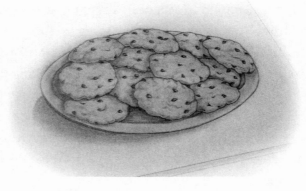

"Oh, Auntie Anne," Kara said, laughing. "I bet you heard that on TV!"

"Well, maybe I did, but I still say that these are mighty fine cookies!"

Mac and Vicki joined in the laughter.

"Mother told me not to stay long because you've

got company," Kara said. "I'll come back another time." Auntie Anne reached out her arms to her young guest. "Maybe you and your mom can drop by later, and we can have some of these with milk."

"Thank you, Auntie Anne!" Kara set Missy down and turned to leave. She hugged Auntie Anne one last time and slipped out the door. Missy slumped and let out a sigh before returning to her padded pillow.

"That was a fun surprise," Mac said, eyeing the cookies.

"Go on. Enjoy one," Auntie Anne said, waving her arm in Mac's direction. "Kara's a good little baker."

"Does she come by often?" Vicki asked.

"Oh, we help each other a lot, little Kara and I. She's a little gift giver."

"It's funny you say that, because our little Emily is always giving gifts. Sometimes it wildflowers or pretty autumn leaves, or a painting she did at school." Vicki rambled on with a few more examples, smiling at her vivid memories of their little gift-giving Emily. Mac was nodding and grinning at his own recollections from 'Emily land'.

They both looked back at Auntie Anne, who was just staring at them, waiting and wondering how much she should tell them. She understood that the mind must be prepared for learning, just as a field must be prepared for planting. A discovery made too soon is often no better than a discovery not made at all.

Mac and Vicki sensed that Auntie Anne was waiting for something to connect.

Mac cleared his throat. "Auntie Anne, gift-giving wouldn't happen to be another way of making honey for our children, would it? Because if it is…" His words trailed off.

Auntie Anne met Mac's intent gaze with an affirming nod, then glanced down to her flowered shift, brushing unseen specks of cookie from her lap. Missy watched, waiting for something big enough to make it worth her while to get up.

"Vicki, every time we come home with a little treat, which one of the kids' faces lights up the most?" Mac asked.

"Emily's."

"And which one is always asking us to buy her something in the store?"

"Emily."

"And which one is always bringing us her drawings as a little gift?"

"Emily."

"Vicki," Mac spoke as an urgent memory lunged

forward, demanding attention. "What did I do with the painting she put on my desk the other day?"

"I don't know. It's probably there somewhere under your stack of mail."

"Clearly it was a gift," Mac said, "but I never even acknowledged it. How could I have missed this too?"

"What did you miss, Mac?" Auntie Anne asked.

"I have a little girl who says 'I love you' with her gift-giving, and I guess—no, I fear—that I have a knack for rejecting her. I don't mean to do it. But it happens so often."

"We both have, Mac," Vicki confessed. "I didn't tell you what she did the other day."

Mac wasn't sure he wanted to hear.

"I opened her lunchbox, and there was a half-eaten brownie wrapped in foil. I learned afterward that she only ate half of it because it was one of those nut-filled brownies I like so much. Emily brought it home to give to me." Forbidden tears began to swell in Vicki's eyes. "I threw it out."

"Man, this parenting stuff would be so much easier if we knew what we were doing," Mac said. "All this time, Emily has been speaking gift-giving to us, and we haven't heard her love language or spoken it back to her. I know one thing—all of that's going to change when we get home."

Auntie Anne smiled as she lifted letters from her tray and placed *verbal* on the board.

Mac broke off a small piece of cookie and reached down beside his chair. "May I, Auntie Anne?" he asked, a moment too late. Missy had already charged toward his dangling hand to accept the love offering. Missy, retrieved the morsel, licked his palm, and retreated to her corner.

~ Saying I Love You Through Words ~

"Come," Auntie Anne said while using the sturdy pine table for support as she stood. "Let's let the board rest for a bit and get some air."

Mac and Vicki followed her out onto the screened in back piazza, which afforded them a wide view of the Wando River. They just stood there and gazed.

A movement in the water caught Vicki's attention. "Look!" Vicki said pointing. "What's that?" Fins were rising and falling in the water in a syncopated rhythm.

"Ahh, the dolphins," Auntie Anne said. "Aren't they lovely? Every day they arrive with the flowing tide."

"What are they doing all together like that?" Vicki whispered, as if the amazing creatures might actually hear her and be frightened away.

"That grouping is called a pod," she said, "and the dolphins are feeding. The pod moves the game fish into tight schools, making it easier for the dolphins to feed. This maneuver works because they know how to communicate in their own special language. They sort of 'talk it through' to get results. No dolphin is left out or behind, and none gets discouraged or feels unimportant."

"Unfortunately, the communication in *our* pod isn't always kind and encouraging," Vicki said. "Heaven knows, some in *our* pod leave much to be desired by way of communication." She continued watching the dolphins, smooth and magnificent until the fins became tiny specks in the distance.

"Are you thinking of the same person I am?" Mac asked her.

Vicki turned to meet his eyes. "Mister Down-in-the Dumps?"

"Jack," they both said nodding simultaneously.

"You know, this is all making sense," Mac started.

Vicki burst in with her thoughts. "It all makes sense, Mac. This whole day has been about making sense. Everything we learn is an amazing revelation." Vicki stopped to catch her breath. "Sorry, Mac. Go on." There was a freedom to her words now, a lighter-than-life openness that came from holding nuggets of truth once out of her reach.

"Remember that incident at the geography bee a few weeks back?" Mac asked. "And how much time Jack put into studying for it? He seemed so disturbed when he came in third. So instead of celebrating, I tried to help him figure out what he could have done better. I remember harping on him a little about some of the things he could have put off in order to have more time to prepare."

"I do remember," Vicki said, lifting her brows. "Jack was so angry that he ended up walking off, mumbling something about homework in his room. Later I saw him slouched on his bed, just looking through an old photo album."

Mac tilted his head to the side, thinking. "Wasn't there supposed to be some writing contest coming up?" he asked. "Whatever happened with that?"

"He never entered," Vicki said. "Just gave up on it I guess. Too much work maybe." She shook her head in confusion.

Auntie Anne was silent. There was no need for her to say anything because so far Mac and Vicki were following the right track on their own.

"What if," Mac began, looking over at Auntie Anne,

"what if I had applauded his success? I mean, third isn't exactly something to feel bad about."

"It's not worthy of shame," Auntie Anne said.

"What was I thinking? All-too-critical Dad. That's me. Always looking to train and change and teach and build, when all I needed to do at that moment was say, 'Hey son, well done!'"

"Build him up, Mac, and he'll give you his best." Auntie Anne smiled as she spoke. "It's not too late to give him what he needs."

"Aha, another language! Right, Auntie Anne?" Vicki said, wanting to give her hurting husband a break. "Words of affirmation. That's one more way to say 'I love you,' isn't it?"

Auntie Anne gave an affirming nod.

"There's something very powerful here," Mac murmured. "Encouraging words, it would seem, motivate. And if that's the case, then the opposite kind of words can devastate some kids," Mac said now enlightened.

"So it is." Auntie Anne said. "Discouraging words can cut deep, especially for the soul that thrives on verbal encouragement."

"That's so like Jack," Vicki said.

"Don't focus on the past, just get busy looking ahead." Auntie Anne reached out a hand resting it on

Mac's shoulder. Her touch encouraged him.

"Those dolphins remind me of a story about good words, words that build up and how they affect all kinds of creatures." Opening the door, Auntie Anne stepped inside knowing that Mac and Vicki would follow. The three slipped into their places at the table. Auntie Anne took a few sips of tea, set her glass down and began her story.

"A group of frogs were blissfully hopping through the woods when two of them fell into a deep pit. All the other frogs gathered around the pit and watched as the imprisoned frogs tried to jump out. The frogs on top could see that there was no way out and started yelling at the frogs below to give up.

'The pit is too deep. You're as good as dead,' the chorus said.

When the trapped frogs kept trying, the crowd yelled louder, 'Give up. You're as good as dead.'

After a while, one of the exhausted frogs took heed of what the others were saying and fell down and died.

"But the second frog kept jumping as hard she could, despite the fact that the others kept on yelling for her to accept the inevitable and die. Finally, with one valiant jump, she made it out of the pit.

You see, this frog was deaf and unable to hear what the others were saying. She thought they were encouraging her the entire time. And that made all the difference."

Auntie Anne picked up a paper napkin from the table, leaned back in her chair, and dabbed at the water drops that had formed on her glass of iced tea.

"As I see it," she said, "the moral of this story is that words can make the difference between success and failure. While time has rendered the author of this delightful tale unknown, the message is clear. Negative words can kill the spirit, but positive words can cause all of us to jump a little higher and try a little harder. Think of what positive words can do for your children."

"I've got a lot of making up to do with Jack," Mac said.

"That may be so," Auntie Anne said. "And you will, every day. Make no mistake about it. You'll have many opportunities to encourage Jack."

"You really think so?" Mac asked.

"A thoughtful word, a courteous response, commending a job well done—all these are good places to start," she replied, smiling. "From there, more will blossom. You can be sure of it."

~ Saying I Love You by Doing ~

The game continued and the letter bag was nearly empty. Mac had been holding on to the *q* for several turns. Now at last he drew the coveted *u*.

"We've got so much to do when we get home," Vicki said. "Of all the love languages you've mentioned, I want to begin with the marsh example. Our kids will get so many hugs, especially R. J. He'll think he's turned into a teddy bear."

"We'll order some rocking chairs before we go home," Mac said. "Becka gets her own special one, and we'll put it right between us."

"And don't forget the frog story," Vicki said. "Maybe we should get a little stuffed frog and keep it in the kitchen to remind us to use encouraging words, especially for Jack. And for sure, we'll arrive home with a special souvenir from Charleston just for Emily."

"We'll be bringing home a whole lot more than gifts this trip. How about two new parents?" Mac's eyes met Vicki's, and together they turned to express their thanks to Auntie Anne.

Auntie Anne responded with a single question. "What about Jillian?"

The game stopped. Mac and Vicki had thought school was out. Auntie Anne paused as the two contemplated what they had missed.

"There's another thing I'll bet you noticed on your drive here," Auntie Anne said, "besides the rockers, I mean. "Down here, in the heart of the low country, everyone's busy doing for others. You can see it in the window boxes down in the historical district, scattered throughout the winding alley ways and cobblestone streets.

"The act of planting the fragrant blooms beautifies

the world for passers-by," she said smiling, breathing in the aroma of this lovely thought. "Window boxes just bursting with colorful begonias and petunias and fragrant hyacinth, with foliage of every imaginable kind. It's all for the eye of the passer-by, an optical feast, if you will. Those fine folks downtown do this because they find pleasure in your satisfaction."

A sly grin appeared on Auntie Anne's lips as she paused momentarily and then shifted the topic. "Who changes the toilet paper roll at your house?" she asked.

Mac raised his eye brows, curious where this was headed.

"By default, mostly me," Vicki said, looking over to

Mac for confirmation. "Wait, Jillian's pretty good about it. In fact, she's always doing little things like that. She's the only child who will start folding laundry without my asking. In fact, I think Jillian is the only child we have who initiates doing things for others."

The light went on in Mac's eyes. "Doing is another love language, isn't it, Auntie Anne?"

"Now I get it," Vicki said. "Whenever you do something for another person that you know they are going to appreciate—even if it's changing the toilet paper roll—you're really saying 'I love you'. Isn't that it, Auntie Anne?"

"Yes, indeed," Auntie Anne said. "And no doubt that little lady likewise delights in the small things you do for her."

"Think back, Vicki," Mac said. "Remember the time you helped her clean her room during finals? She talked about that for days. Oh, and the time I washed her bike after the ride she took on that muddy trail. You would have thought I had bought her a new one. She was so appreciative."

"Now that you mention it Mac, those are the times when I see true twinges of joy in that child. The only other time might be when she takes my broom and sweeps off the front walk. I just thought that was a game for her, so I never made a big deal about it."

"Oh, no." All of a sudden Mac's countenance changed. "Remember the picnic basket Jillian packed for our trip here?"

"Ohhh, I do." Vicki frowned. "We were all over her for not asking us first and for using up a week's supply of sandwich stuff. That poor child, Mac, she must have been crushed. We just pulled away, all wrapped up in getting to Charleston." Vicki let her head fall into her propped-up hands, and tears began running down her cheeks.

Auntie Anne patted her arm with one hand and reached into her apron pocket for a clean hanky with the other.

"Jillian does the same kinds of things for her siblings," Mac said. "Vicki, do you remember those folded paper toys she was making for a while?" He stroked Vicki's hand.

"Origami," Vicki said, wiping her eyes.

"That's it. The other kids loved it, and Jillian got the biggest kick out of seeing them play with her creations."

"We have missed so much," Vicki said. She paused for a moment, "Oh, this conversation reminds me of someone who is always filling up my gas tank for the week, and I just take it for granted." She turned her hand over in Mac's and looked into his eyes. "Can you forgive me for not appreciating your thoughtfulness, Hon? I guess I'm just not tuned in to that sort of thing. But I know I need to be."

"I forgive you for all of it." Mac laughed.

"What do you mean, 'all of it'?"

"Well, making the coffee every morning and throwing in some laundry now and again. You know all those wonderful extra things I do around the house as a perfect husband," Mac said with an impish look.

At this, they all had a hearty laugh.

Still smiling, Mac turned his attention to the board. He pondered for a moment and added *quiz*, thankful not to be stuck with the *q* or *z*. It mattered little. Auntie

Anne ended the game by using her last two letters. She added the scores, subtracted Vicki and Mac's leftover letters, and then carefully poured the golden brown tiles back into the blue velvet bag.

"The verdict Auntie Anne?" Mac asked.

"Well Vicki trailed you by a few points and you trailed me by twenty-two-points."

"I thought so," Mac said resigning himself to second place. "But I want a rematch someday. Promise me Auntie Anne?"

"I'll look forward to it," she said while pushing back from the table. She rose and crossed the room.

Missy snatched her squeaky ball in her mouth and began trailing after Auntie Anne. The sound of the squeak prompted her to stop and turn.

"Oh, you want to play, do you? Here then, hand it to me," she said. Missy chewed on the ball a couple of times and then dropped it. Auntie Anne bent over and with a single motion picked up the ball and tossed it into the great room. Missy ran after it. With her little legs churning and her nails clicking on the smooth hardwood floors, she slid right past the ball.

Meanwhile, Auntie Anne opened the cupboard and pulled out a small square decorative tin. She carried it to the table, set it down, and removed the lid. Inside were newspaper clippings, pages from magazines, copies of recipes, and handwritten notes, all saved for posterity. Auntie Anne sorted through the contents. "Oh, here it is," she said. "I've been holding on to this one. Miss Vicki, you and Mr. Mac take it home and make some copies."

Vicki unfolded the two pages. At the top of the first one was the title, "Love Language Test," followed by the instructions.

"That will make for a fun family night," Auntie Anne said, "and it will help you and your children remember all the different ways to say 'I love you.'"

Mac leaned way back in his chair, ran his hands through his thick crop of dark hair, and folded his fingers together at the back of his head. A myriad of thoughts ran through him. *What if I hadn't come? The things I would have missed. Her words brought comfort. Now I'm leaving a richer man, with wisdom and purpose. I once loved my children with random acts of love. Now I can direct my love and every day fill their hearts with what they need. Make honey...* Mac thought. *Keep your bees at home.*

"So, realistically Auntie Anne, I have five different primary approaches operating in my home on any single day." Mac spoke softly, trying to deal with his new awareness.

"Quite so," Auntie Anne said. "But it isn't enough

to just know how to say 'I love you' to all of them in their own unique languages. It isn't even enough to get them to speak each other's primary love language. That's important, all right, but the real task is something much more basic."

Auntie Anne signaled for Vicki and Mac to follow her. Her room had a door opening onto a bright sunlit porch decorated with tan wicker chairs and a glass-top coffee table displaying a large red geranium bursting with blooms.

Auntie Anne pointed up. "Look under the eaves right there. Do you see the swallow's nest? See the three bobbing heads? I love to watch their parents come and go. I've watched them since they brought the first twigs and dabs of mud for the nest, and now their babies are just about ready to fly. Loving those chicks was their priority, and they nurtured them every day without fail. They never rested from their toil or closed their eyes to their offspring's needs."

She turned to Mac and Vicki. "How is it that these creatures know what we humans should do?" She paused for a moment, stared at the nest and then back to her guest.

"The human heart, Mac and Vicki, has a hole in it, one that surgeons can not fix. Every day it leaks love, so every day it has to be refilled. When it comes to mankind, love is a choice. Every day we can choose to love, and every day we can choose not to love. That is why, every day, we must all choose to say 'I love you' to those around us. We must put honey out for them to feed on. *That's* a fundamental task of parenting."

Auntie Anne turned and made her way back to the kitchen. Mac and Vicki stared up at the nest then followed their mentor out. The time had come to say good-bye. With tearful embraces and words of farewell, Mac and Vicki took their leave of Auntie Anne.

The sun was high just beginning its movement toward the afternoon sky. Mac and Vicki descended the front steps slowly, pausing once to turn and wave. It had been one of those marvelous once-in-a-lifetime days never lost to memory. Vague feelings of being forever indebted to this treasure of a woman flooded their minds. They were debtors to her wisdom. How would they explain this day to the carriage couples, who anxiously awaited their report? The whole experience was a mystery, even to Mac and Vicki. But they did know this: If fear was the thief that stole their hope, Auntie Anne was the benefactor who had restored it.

"Let's go home and see the kids, Vicki," Mac said. "We have some honey to make!"

Bringing it Home
Questions for the Heart

1. In this story, Auntie Anne used a bee and honey analogy. In your own words briefly explain the 'honey' principle as it relates to your children.

2. Please describe the general premise of Auntie Anne's Love language teaching?

3. Auntie Anne explained to Mac and Vicki that "the human heart has a hole in it." What point was she stressing?

4. Do you know your own primary emotional language?

Mac and Vicki took this exercise home and shared it with their children. Try it in your family. Below are five groupings of five statements. Read the sentences within each group and then score each on a 5-1 scale, with 5 being the statement that most makes you (or child feel loved). Use each number only once within each group. Also note that some questions distinguish between male and female. Answer these questions according to your gender and position in the family.

Group One

A. ____ Your spouse/child says, "You really did a great job with that. I appreciate it."

B. ____ Your spouse/child unexpectedly does something in or around the house or your room that you appreciate.

C. ____ Your spouse/child brings you home a surprise treat from the store.

D. ____ Your spouse/child invites you to go on a leisurely walk just to chat.

E. ____ Your spouse/child makes it a point to embrace and kiss you before leaving the house.

Group Two

A. ____ Your spouse/child tells you how much he or she appreciates you.

B. ____ Your spouse/child (male) volunteers to do the dishes and encourages you to relax. Your spouse/child (female) volunteers to wash your car and encourages you to relax.

C. ____ Your spouse/child (male) brings you flowers, just because he cares. Your spouse/child (female) brings you home a special food treat from the local bakery.

D. ____ Your spouse/child invites you to sit down and talk about your day.

E. ____ Your spouse/child gives you a hug even when you are just passing by room to room.

Group Three

A. ____ During a party, your spouse/child shares about a recent success you had.

B. ____ Your spouse/child cleans out your car.

C. ____ Your spouse/child surprises you with an unexpected gift.

D. ____ Your spouse/child surprises you with a special after-noon trip.

E. ____ Your spouse holds your hand as you walk through the mall, or your child/parent stands by your side with an arm around your shoulder at a public event.

Group Four

A. ____ Your spouse/child praises you about one of your special qualities.

B. ____ Your spouse/child brings you breakfast in bed.

C. ____ Your spouse/child surprises you with a membership to something you always wanted.

D. ____ Your spouse/child plans a special night out for the two of you.

E. ____ Your spouse/child will personally drive you to an event instead of you having to go on the old, crowded bus with the team.

Group Five

A. ____ Your spouse/child tells you how much his or her friends appreciate you.

B. ____ Your spouse/child takes the time to fill out the long, complicated applications you had hoped to get to this evening.

C. ____ Your spouse/child sends you something special through the mail.

D. ____ Your spouse/child kidnaps you for lunch and takes you to your favorite restaurant.

E. ___   Your spouse/child gives you a massage.

Now transfer your scores from each test questions to the scoring profile. Then add up each column for a total score per each love language.

Score Profile

	Encouraging Words	Acts of Service	Gift-Giving	Quality Time	Touch
Group 1	A____	B____	C____	D____	E____
Group 2	A____	B____	C____	D____	E____
Group 3	A____	B____	C____	D____	E____
Group 4	A____	B____	C____	D____	E____
Group 5	A____	B____	C____	D____	E____
Totals	A____	B____	C____	D____	E____

This test measures how you primarily desire to receive love and will also indicate how you probably find yourself expressing love more often. Compare your score with your spouse/child/parent. Write down from the greatest to the least the love languages of each family member.

1._____

2._____

3._____

4._____

5._____